WHALES!
The Gentle Giants

Robyn P. Watts

KNOWLEDGE
BOOKS

Teacher Notes:

Whales, dolphins, and porpoises are some of the most important and fascinating mammals living in the oceans and rivers of our world. Join the author as she discovers where whales came from, what they eat, where they migrate, and why we need to do everything we can to protect them.

Discussion points for consideration:

1. What types of whales, dolphins, and porpoises live in your part of the world?

2. Why is it important to try and save all the Cetaceans from extinction?

3. Why is the whale watching industry so important to both people and whales?

Difficult words to be introduced and practiced before reading this book:

Porpoise, dolphin, Cetaceans, California, extinct, Vaquita, scientists, Amazon, echolocation, temperature, mammals, disappeared, amazing, ancestors, surface, baleen, sieve, filter, crustaceans, algae, carbon dioxide, fertilize , migration, routes, America, Australia, journey, Antarctica, identified, environment.

Contents

1. What are Whales?

Whales, porpoises, and dolphins are special animals. Whales are Cetaceans. Some Cetaceans are the largest animals on Earth.

The Blue Whale can be over 100 feet long. Cetaceans can weigh up to 100 tons. This is about the same size as 60 SUVs!

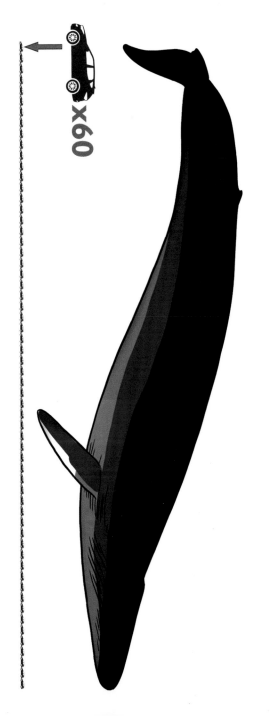

Some Cetaceans are very small whales. These small whales are also important for the oceans. The smallest porpoise is a Vaquita. The Vaquita lives in the Gulf of California. There are only 10 to 20 Vaquita left in the world. It needs to be saved before it becomes extinct.

Humans can help the Vaquita by not fishing with gill nets where the Vaquita live. We also need to protect their food. Scientists need to study the Vaquita to see if they can live safely in other waters. How would you try to save the Vaquita?

How can we save the little Vaquita?

Whales, dolphins, and porpoises are found in oceans and rivers all over the world. The smaller ones often live in rivers. Many types of dolphins live only in rivers.

The Amazon River has its own dolphins. Dolphins also live in the Ganges River in India. These dolphins are blind. They find fish by bouncing off sounds. This is called echolocation.

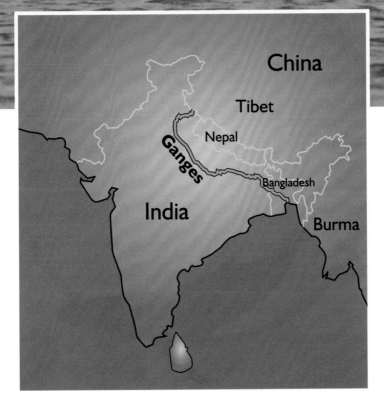

2. What Did Whales Come From?

The first whales were small land mammals that looked a bit like a deer. Over millions of years, they changed into giant sea mammals. Fossils from this time show these changes.

The early fossils show mammals that lived partly in water. Later fossils show how their limbs changed to form flippers. The back legs disappeared, leaving just a small bone. Scientists believe that all Cetaceans came from this small deer-like mammal.

The best way to see changes over millions of years is to look at a whale's flipper. Here, you can see the same bones as a land mammal. These include small bones from fingers and from limbs. These bones grew to form a flipper for swimming instead of a limb for running.

What happened to the back legs and hip bones of the whale? This is also amazing! There are tiny bones near a whale's tail. These bones were once part of the back legs and hip bone of the early whales.

3. Whales are Mammals

When we study mammals, we know these facts about them:

a. They give birth to live young (they do not hatch from an egg).

b. They have hair on their skin.

c. They make milk for their young.

d. They are warm-blooded (their temperature stays the same).

e. They breathe air into lungs (they do not have gills like fish).

Are whales really mammals? Do you agree with all these facts?

The ancestors of whales were mammals. Whales, porpoises, and dolphins – the Cetaceans – are all mammals for these reasons:

a. Whales give birth to live young. The mother whale comes to the surface during birth. She releases the baby and nudges it up to breathe air.

b. Whales breathe air through the hole in their skull. They must come to the surface for air.

c. Whales swim easily with their smooth skin. They have small patches of hair on their head and near their lips. Some whales have more hair than others.

d. The mother whale feeds the calf milk. The calf bumps the mother and the milk flows. The calf grows quickly on the milk.

e. Whales have warm blood like a mammal. Their blood is not the temperature of the water. They keep warm by eating lots of food. The layer of meat and fat helps to keep them warm.

4. What Do Whales Eat?

Most of the giant whales have no teeth. They are baleen whales. The baleen works like a sieve. It scoops up the krill that are floating in the ocean.

The whale takes a huge mouthful of krill and salt water. It strains the water out through the baleen. It then eats the krill that is left over. Whales need tons of krill to survive!

Some of the giant whales live in the polar areas. Massive balls of krill swim in these waters. The whales fill up on krill to grow bigger and stronger.

17

Krill are small crustaceans. They look like a small prawn or shrimp. They eat floating plants like algae. They also eat tiny eggs from other critters.

The algae have carbon dioxide in their cells. When krill eat algae, they also take the carbon dioxide. Krill help reduce the carbon dioxide in our oceans. When whales eat the krill, their poop helps to fertilize the algae.

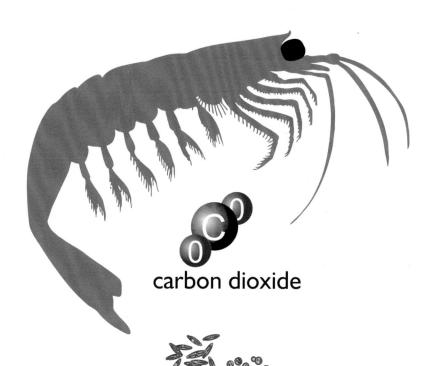

carbon dioxide

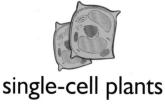

phytoplankton

green algae

single-cell plants

Whales that have teeth eat other foods. Some whales have large teeth. They can attack and kill fish, seals, sharks, and other whales.

Orcas or Killer Whales are ocean hunters. Orcas can hunt many other sea animals. They hunt in packs and are very clever. This makes them deadly!

Bats use echolocation to help find objects in the air. Dolphins, porpoises, and whales use the same echolocation skills. The only difference is that they do this in the water.

The dolphin or porpoise makes clicking sounds. These clicking sounds bounce off things in the water. This sound bounce gives them a map of where fish are hiding. This helps them find their food.

Dolphins are very clever at finding food. They work together with other dolphins to catch fish. They have even been known to work with humans to move fish into nets.

When dolphins are searching for fish to eat, they work together in their pod. First, they chase the fish into a tight ball. Then, they catch the fish on the edge of the big fish ball. They keep doing this until the ball of fish breaks up again.

5. Where Do Whales Go?

Many whales travel great distances each year. Some come from the polar areas to warm areas to have their babies. Every year, whales travel thousands of miles. This is called migration.

They leave the icy polar waters and move to warmer waters. The warmer water gives their babies a better chance of surviving.

Whales have many different migration routes across the world. Some whales travel along the coasts of South and North America. They move from the cold polar waters to the warmer oceans.

Whales also travel up the East coast of Australia. Every year, they migrate to the warm waters off Queensland. Here, they will have their babies and rest up before the journey back to Antarctica.

6. Can Whales Talk?

Whales make a lot of noise in the oceans. They make the loudest sounds of all animals. Other whales can hear the sounds from hundreds of miles away. Sound in water travels faster than in the air. Whales talk over long distances to find each other.

Whales have long songs that they sing to each other in the pod. These whale sounds are special for each whale. A whale can be identified by its whale song.

7. Looking After Whales

We all need to protect whales to make sure they survive. These days, many countries have laws to help protect whales. However, it was not always like this.

In the past, many countries hunted whales. Some whales almost became extinct because of this hunting. These days, whales are safe from hunting across most of the world. Only a small number of people still eat whale meat and whale numbers are still growing.

Whale watching is very popular. Many people take tour boats to watch the whales. Sometimes they come right out of the water and make a huge splash. They can be very playful. It is important that the tour boats follow the rules and give the whales their space.

During a whale watching tour, you can often see whole whale families together. There might be moms, aunties, babies, sisters, and brothers swimming together. The whales stay together on these long trips. They protect one another.

The little whales and river dolphins also need our help. Many of the rivers across the world are becoming very polluted. Poisons in rivers can kill fish and dolphins. It also takes away their food. This has happened because humans have not been looking after the environment.

The Yangtze River Dolphin in China is now extinct. It has not been seen in 30 years.

8. Why We Need Whales

As we know, krill eat lots of algae in the oceans. The whales then eat the krill. The whales help to fertilize the algae with their poop. This whole cycle helps to keep carbon dioxide levels down in our oceans. This helps to slow down climate change.

Scientists are studying the importance of whales and dolphins in our world. They have found that the Cetaceans help to keep our oceans clean and healthy. If the ocean is healthy, then more creatures are healthy. This is good for the whole food web.

WHALE FOOD CYCLE

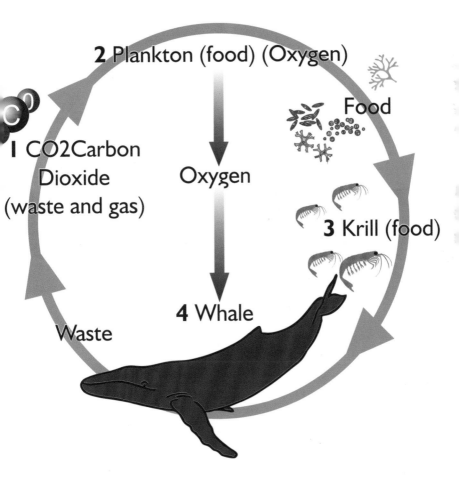

As a young girl, I was fishing in a bay with my grandfather. We were in a little rowboat. Suddenly, I heard a large gasp of air that sounded like a giant cow.

I looked into the water to see something like a submarine below the boat. I was scared but my grandfather told me it was only a whale and it knew who was above.

It was the biggest thing I have seen. It glided carefully under the boat and dived into the dark water. I will never forget this encounter.

Whales are intelligent mammals. They are amazing to watch. They bring joy and wonder to everyone.

Is it better that they live in our oceans or should they be hunted?

All Cetaceans across the world need our help. Many of the river dolphins are finding it hard to survive. The world would be a lot worse off without these beautiful animals.

Here are some ways we can support whales:

a. talk about them with friends.

b. read about them online and leave comments online.

c. start a topic on your favourite page.

d. write a letter to your government.

What other ways can you help? Let's look after these amazing mammals, big and small. Let's keep their future safe!

Word Bank

porpoise

dolphin

Cetaceans

California

extinct

Vaquita

scientists

Amazon

echolocation

temperature

mammals

disappeared

amazing

ancestors

surface

baleen

sieve

filter

crustaceans

algae

carbon dioxide

fertilize

migration

routes

America

Australia

journey

Antarctica

identified

environment